THE HISTORY DETECTIVE INVESTIGATES

VICTORIAN SCHOOL

Richard Wood

HAMILTON COLLEGE LIBRARY

Wayland

an imprint of Hodder Children's Books

The History Detective series
Tudor Home
Tudor Medicine
Tudor Theatre
Tudor War
Victorian Crime
Victorian Factory
Victorian School
Victorian Transport

First published in Great Britain in 2002 by Hodder Wayland,
an imprint of Hodder Children's Books
© Copyright 2002 Hodder Wayland
This paperback edition published in 2003

Hodder Children's Books
A division of Hodder Headline Limited
338 Euston Road, London NW1 3BH

Editor: Kay Barnham
Designer: Simon Borrough
Cartoon artwork: Richard Hook
Picture research: Shelley Noronha – Glass Onion Pictures

British Library Cataloguing in Publication Data

Wood, Richard, 1949-
    The history detective investigates a Victorian school
    1. Schools – Great Britain – History – 19th century –
    Juvenile literature
    2. Great Britain – social conditions – 19th century –
    Juvenile literature
    I. Title II. A Victorian school
    371'.00941'09034

ISBN: 0 7502 3744 9

Printed and bound in Italy by G. Canale & C.S.p.A., Turin

Picture acknowledgements:
The publishers would like to thank the following for
permission to reproduce their pictures: Armley Mill 21
(bottom); Barnham Broom Primary School 24; BEAMISH
The North of England Open Air Museum 13 (bottom), 21
(top); Billie Love Historical Pictures 8 (bottom), 9 (top and
bottom), 14 (bottom), 18; Greater London Photo Library 26,
27 (top); Hulton Deutsch 27 (bottom); Hulton Getty 7
(top), 16 (bottom), 19 (left); Mary Evans Picture Library 1, 5,
6 (bottom), 12 (top and bottom), 15 (bottom), 25 (bottom)
front cover (4 pictures), *back cover* (2 pictures); Norfolk
Museums and Archaeology Service/WPL 7 (bottom), *front
cover* (2 pictures); Public Record Office 15 (bottom), 20
(bottom); Punch 23 (top); Richard Wood 11 (right), 28, 29;
Wayland Picture Library 4, 5 (top), 8 (middle), 10, 11 (left),
13 (top), 14 (top), 15 (top), 16 (top), 17, 19 (right), 20 (top),
21 (bottom), 22, 23 (top and bottom), 24, 25 (top), *back
cover* (1 picture); Wicklewood Primary School 11 (right).

CONTENTS

WHO WENT TO SCHOOL IN VICTORIAN TIMES?

Imagine that you did not have to go to school… Wouldn't this be strange? But, when Queen Victoria's reign began in 1837, 40 per cent of children never attended school – and those who did rarely stayed long enough even to learn how to read and write. A government report said that only one in ten children received an 'adequate' education. Why was this? In this book, history detective Sherlock Bones will help you to discover what Victorian schools were like and how they gradually changed.

When Sherlock started his investigation, he soon found out that the sort of education Victorian children received usually depended on how much money their families had. Rich parents sent their sons to famous boarding schools, such as Eton and Winchester, while their daughters were taught at home. Middle-class children went to private schools, sometimes run by teachers in their own homes.

But, for poor children, there was often no school at all. Some people even said it was wrong for them to go to school. They did not need 'book learning' to do simple jobs, and schooling might make them unhappy and hard to control. But gradually, people's attitudes changed. They realized that having well-educated workers would help make the whole country richer. From 1833, governments began spending taxpayers' money to help schools. Eventually, in 1880, schooling became compulsory for all children between the ages of five and ten.

Ragged children make fun of a Sunday school scholar.

There is a lot to discover about what life was like at school. Sherlock Bones will help you to find clues in old photos, record books, local directories, buildings – perhaps even in your own school. You should then be able to find enough evidence to present a project on a part of Victorian school life. Sherlock's own project is to find out about workhouse schools. You can see what he discovers on page 29.

Wherever you see one of Sherlock's pawprints, like this, you will find a puzzle to solve. The answers are on pages 30 and 31.

✿ Compare the two pictures on this page. What made these two schools so different?

Poor children exercising in their classroom at a London school.

Teachers, known as 'beaks', welcome new boys to Eton College.

DID PARENTS HAVE TO PAY?

Victorian parents expected to pay something for their children's education. Even 'free' schools, like charity, church and Sunday schools asked parents to make regular donations to help pay the teacher and buy books. The cheapest education was often at a 'dame school', run by an old lady in a cottage. The teaching may have been poor, but the charge was only a few pence a week.

Children of all ages went to the village dame school.

Most towns had a variety of small private schools, each taking thirty or forty pupils. These were businesses, often run by teachers in their own homes. Children from country districts paid extra to board with the family during the week. These schools were usually single sex. Victorians believed that boys and girls had totally different abilities and needs. So, except when they were very young, they were taught separately.

Private schools were not supervised by the government and conditions could be bad. Sometimes children were ill-fed and cruelly treated, as at Dotheboys Hall, the fictional school in Charles Dickens' novel *Nicholas Nickleby*.

❖ What shows that the lady held the school in her home?

❖ Does the furniture look suitable for use in a school?

For older pupils, grammar and public schools provided the best education, though they were usually so expensive that only rich families could afford the fees. These schools concentrated on the 'classics' – Latin and Greek language and literature – which pupils had to learn to get into university or a profession like law or the church. This did not suit everyone. Winston Churchill, the great English wartime prime minister, could not cope with the classical education at Harrow, and left without any qualifications.

Private schools encouraged sports. This was the Tonbridge School cricket team in about 1865.

DETECTIVE WORK

Find out about local private schools today – were they in existence in Victorian times? Who founded them? What sort of people went there? Did they take girls and boys? In your local library or Record Office, look in the Victorian county directories for the names of private schools in your area.

The advert on the right lists the fees at a small private school. There are extra charges for French, music and drawing.

Subjects like maths, history and even science were also taught in grammar and public schools, but not English – pupils were expected to know this already. These schools were just for boys. However, by late Victorian times, some new grammar and public schools for girls were opened. The Victorians had at last realized that girls had brains too!

No. 4, CORONATION SQUARE.

MRS. STEWART,

WIDOW OF THE LATE REV. EBENEZER STEWART,

Begs to inform her Friends and the Public, that for the benefit of her rising family, she purposes receiving Pupils to educate with them, on the following terms.

	per Quarter. £. s. d.
Day Pupils instructed in the different branches of an English Education, including Writing, and Arithmetic.............................	0 15 0
Pupils under eight years of age...............	0 8 0

	per Annum. £. s. d.
Day Boarders	10 0 0

	per Quarter. £. s. d.
French and Music, (each)	0 15 0
Drawing,.................................	0 10 0

*** The School will be opened on Monday, July the 9th.

MRS. S. confidently hopes by unremitting attention to the moral and intellectual improvement of the Children committed to her charge, to merit that share of patronage which she now respectfully solicits.

July, 1832.

Gilbert, High Street, Lynn.

WERE ANY SCHOOLS FREE?

Most Victorian schools charged fees of some sort. But for the poorest, schooling was free. Workhouse children had to attend lessons every morning. People hoped that school would give them a good start in life, so that they would be able to find work later. In larger towns, free schools taught the children of less 'respectable' poor families. Ragged schools, as they were called, had a hard time as the children were so dirty and unruly. Many did not last long.

At ragged schools, pupils had to study the pictures shown below. Each small picture had a number. When the teacher called the number, the pupil had to sit or stand like that particular picture.

❖ Look at the line of figures below. How many different activities can you see?

❖ What does the picture tell us about discipline in Victorian schools?

Children in a ragged school in 1894. Some had no shoes.

Since the 1780s, many churches and chapels had run Sunday schools to teach children how to read the Bible. Later on, they opened weekday schools for poorer children, too – usually called 'national' or 'British' schools. Parents were expected to pay a few pence each week, though most school costs were paid by better-off church members. Even so, these schools had to be run as cheaply as possible. Older pupils called monitors did much of the teaching. The teacher taught the monitors, then the monitors taught groups of children. This way, one adult teacher could direct a hundred or more pupils.

A village school.

From the 1830s, the government began to grant money to help these schools. But, in return, they had to follow government rules and be inspected every year. In 1870, a new Act of Parliament said that school places must be available for all children under ten. If the churches could not provide them, money must be raised from the rates (a local tax) to found a 'board school'. This was run by an elected 'board' of local people.

Fees, called 'schools pence', still had to be paid, though this was not compulsory after 1891.

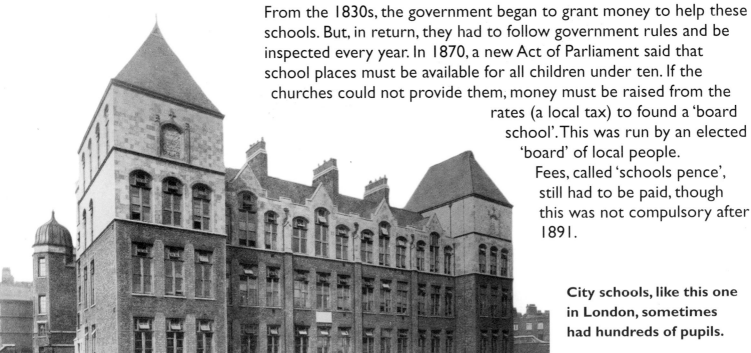

City schools, like this one in London, sometimes had hundreds of pupils.

DID VICTORIANS WANT TO GO TO SCHOOL?

Nobody today would seriously suggest that school is a waste of time. Yet that was the honest view of some Victorian people. Many children did not want to go to school. They did not like sitting in rows of desks learning lessons under the eye of a stern teacher. They felt that 'book work' was of no benefit to the simple farm or factory jobs they hoped to do.

This teacher brightened up her classroom with displays of pupils' work on the walls.

More importantly, if children were in school they could not work. There were no state benefits in Victorian times, and many families relied on their children's wages just to survive. When schooling became compulsory, parents often resented the schools pence fees, and refused to pay. Some parents would physically assault teachers rather than pay up. Rich people had other worries. They thought that if the poor were educated, they would read books filled with 'dangerous' ideas that criticized the ruling classes. They would become unhappy with their lives and try to better themselves by overthrowing the government.

But Victorian Britain was changing fast. Inventions and discoveries made working life much more complicated. People needed to be able to read instructions to operate new machines. When working men were given the vote in 1867, politicians recognized that they needed to read to understand the ideas they were voting for. Governments tried to improve first the quantity, then the quality of schools. They replaced the monitors with older 'pupil teachers', founded new colleges to train teachers properly, tried to improve school buildings and opened 'technical schools' for older pupils. Finally, in 1899, they raised the school-leaving age from 10 to 12.

☙ Compare the two teachers shown on these pages. What made their methods different?

☙ Which teacher do you think got the best work out of their pupils?

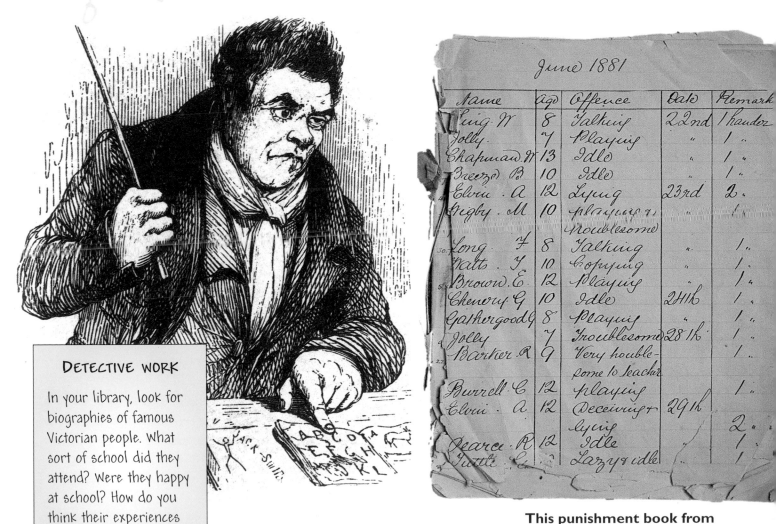

DETECTIVE WORK

In your library, look for biographies of famous Victorian people. What sort of school did they attend? Were they happy at school? How do you think their experiences of school affected the rest of their lives?

This frowning schoolmaster hit children who could not name letters of the alphabet.

This punishment book from Wicklewood School records how many times a pupil was hit for each offence.

WHAT HAPPENED IF PUPILS WERE NAUGHTY?

This 'dunce' stands on a box for all to see.

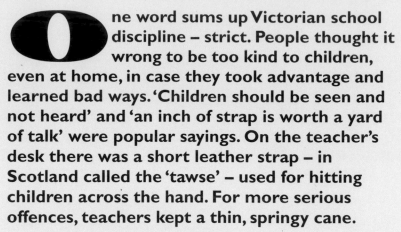

One word sums up Victorian school discipline – strict. People thought it wrong to be too kind to children, even at home, in case they took advantage and learned bad ways. 'Children should be seen and not heard' and 'an inch of strap is worth a yard of talk' were popular sayings. On the teacher's desk there was a short leather strap – in Scotland called the 'tawse' – used for hitting children across the hand. For more serious offences, teachers kept a thin, springy cane.

As well as being punished for bad behaviour, children were also beaten for spelling mistakes, forgetting their times tables or making ink blots on their books. As punishment for poor work, children stood in the corner wearing a 'dunce's hat'. The hat made children feel foolish – some feared it more than the cane. But there were rewards, too. Good work could win points or stars. At the end of the year, those who had worked the hardest might be given a certificate or win a book. Those who never missed school were rewarded with medals.

The teacher watches anxiously while an inspector tests the children.

There was a lot of pressure to do well. Instead of being divided into year groups by age, children at most Victorian schools were placed in 'standards'. The higher the standard, the more difficult the work. At the end of the year, an inspector tested the children. If they failed their standard, they had to repeat the whole year. This often meant that older children were in the same class as much younger children.

This certificate, signed by the vicar, was a reward for good religious knowledge.

Standard Four Examination 1890 *(usually age nine)*

Reading: Read a passage from a reading book or history of England.
Writing: Accurately write down eight lines of poetry when dictated by the teacher. Show copy-books to inspector.
Arithmetic: Compound rules (money) and reduction of weights and measures.

❋ Which parts of the test would modern-day children find most difficult?

❋ Did the inspector see every child individually?

Teachers were under pressure, too. In 1862, a system called 'payment by results' was introduced. If their pupils' test results were poor, teachers had their wages cut. This was very unfair on teachers in schools in poor areas. The worst teachers ended up in the poorest schools, which helped nobody. Eventually, in 1897, the system was abolished.

A wooden strap, designed especially for hitting children hard across the hand.

DETECTIVE WORK

Look for school stories in old books, magazines or comics. The characters may be fictional, but the sorts of rewards and punishments described were probably based on fact.

WHAT SCHOOL RULES DID THEY HAVE?

Do you have school rules? They are usually common sense rules – such as walking instead of running in corridors. Victorian schools were very keen on rules, and children had to learn them by heart. Any child who broke the rules risked being caned. Pupils who broke the rules often might even be expelled. Parents were warned of this, and had to agree to a school's rules before their children were admitted.

You will see from the school rules on page 15 that these had to be obeyed even when pupils were not at school. If they saw a 'better class' of person, such as a doctor or a vicar's wife, boys had to raise their hats and girls had to curtsey. If they did not, pupils would be reported to their teacher and punished. Most Victorian schools belonged to church organizations. That is why they often had rules about kindness, honesty and truth – and about going to church on Sundays! However, there were no rules about uniform. Schools did not usually have uniforms in Victorian times, though pupils were expected to be clean and tidy.

Checking children's hair for lice. School health inspectors tried to prevent the spread of illness.

Children singing in church. Some schools insisted that all their pupils attend church.

Brooke National School Rules, 1839.

Children are:
* *to behave respectfully to the mistresses, managers and visitors and to be lowly and reverent to their betters, both in school and whenever they meet them elsewhere.*
* *to come with their hands and faces well washed, their hair clean and neat, and never be without pocket handkerchiefs.*
* *to be kind to their school fellows and to all other children, and to avoid all quarrelling.*
* *never to mock cripples or infirm persons, nor be rude to the old.*
* *to keep holy the Sabbath, and to behave with seriousness, attention and reverence in all places of public worship.*
* *on all occasions to speak the TRUTH.*
* *to be quiet in school, not to use any play things in school time, to keep their books neat and free from dog's ears, and not to climb upon the desks nor to scrawl upon or damage the desks, forms or walls of the school house.*

Of course, despite the rules, Victorian children still misbehaved sometimes. The rules shown here will tell you some of the things they did wrong. If Victorian pupils did not misbehave, there would have been no need for rules in the first place!

❧ Why do you think children had to have pocket handkerchiefs?

❧ The Brooke School rules mention dog's ears. Do they mean a real dog's ears?

This cube puzzle has six Bible illustrations to assemble.

DETECTIVE WORK

DETECTIVE WORK

Copy down your school rules. Are any of them the same as the Victorian rules? Which ones are different? Ask some older people if they remember any rules from their schooldays. These may not have changed much since Victorian times.

Some schools taught girls domestic skills, like washing and ironing. This would help them to find work as servants.

WAS IT EASY BEING A TEACHER?

SCHOOL TEACHER.
*Of all the Dunces in the School,
You are indeed the greatest fool.*

Some people say that in Victorian times teachers had a good job and were respected by everyone. But this was not always so, and for many teachers life was very hard. Sometimes there was no proper schoolroom, and they had to teach in a converted barn or a space at the back of the church. After 1862, head teachers had to keep log books. These show that schools were often overcrowded and cold, with badly behaved children and difficult parents. Some teachers took boxing lessons so that they could defend themselves if they were attacked by angry parents.

This rude valentine card shows children making fun of their teacher.

Class sizes were often huge, as at this board school in 1876.

Teachers' wages were low. There were no fixed rates of pay, and small country schools often paid teachers less than £1 per week. Men always earned more than women, and sometimes they lived in a house next to the classrooms for free. But this was a mixed blessing. There was little escape from school and holidays were short – two weeks at Christmas, one week at Easter and four weeks in August or September during harvest time.

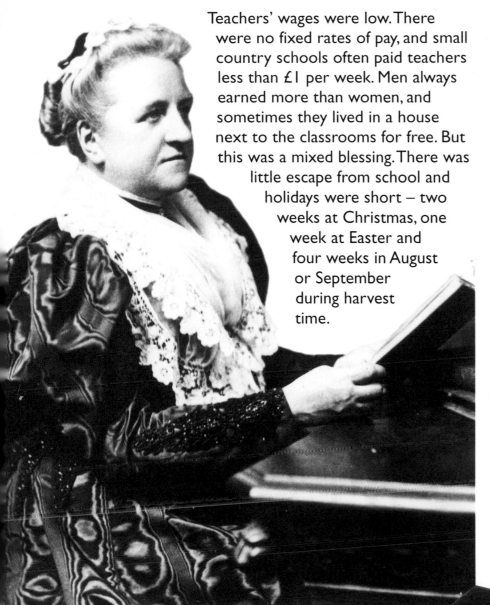

This grand-looking lady taught at Cheltenham Ladies' College.

> ### Extract from Wicklewood School Log Book, 1 July 1879
>
> *Mary Ann Turner (a pupil teacher) is a very poor disciplinarian – she does not seem to possess any tact for management – I put her with the 3rd standard the other afternoon and I was obliged to cane one boy rather more than usual, through the disorder in her class, and this afternoon when I spoke to her about sending out 9 boys out of 38, she answered me very insolently and tossed her head and replied in a very impudent tone, 'Oh! I can leave, if that won't do.'*

✿ What do the pictures and log book extract tell you about life as a Victorian teacher?

Teachers at grammar schools had usually studied at university, but had no special teacher training. Some teachers at elementary school had studied for a teacher's certificate at college. However, many younger pupils were taught by teenage 'pupil teachers', who were paid only a few shillings a week. One organization said that the main teaching qualifications were, 'to be of meek temper and humble behaviour, to have a good government of themselves, and to keep good order'.

DETECTIVE WORK

If your school is old, your head teacher may still have Victorian teachers' log books. Ask if you can see them. Does your local library have histories of schools in your area? These may contain quotes from log books, and stories about the teachers and pupils.

WHAT WERE VICTORIAN CLASSROOMS LIKE?

A class of well-behaved girls and their teacher in a Victorian school.

DETECTIVE WORK

Maybe your school still uses old Victorian buildings. If not, see if you can visit an old school, or look at some of the photos in this book. What were Victorian classrooms like?

Some modern schools still use nineteenth-century buildings – but there is a big difference in how the rooms are used. Early Victorian classrooms were often in homes, halls, churches or barns. Later on, purpose-built classrooms were provided, and these tended to follow a similar pattern. Bigger schools had a hall in the centre. From this, glazed doors led into separate classrooms, one for each 'standard'. The head teacher could keep an eye on all of the classes. Windows were high up to stop the children being distracted by the outside world. Small country schools with just a single classroom had desks arranged in blocks, one for each 'standard'.

Today's classrooms often have tables joined so that pupils can work together in groups. The opposite was the case for Victorians. Children were forbidden to talk to each other in class. Desks were in rows, all facing the teacher. In smaller elementary schools, boys and girls were taught together. But they did not sit together. Oh no! The boys sat on one side of the room, the girls on the other. They even went in and out of the classroom through separate doors and played in separate playgrounds at opposite ends of the school.

The teacher taught older boys (called monitors) who then taught younger ones.

The blackboard and teacher's desk stood at the front of the classroom, raised up on a platform so that the teacher could keep a beady eye on the pupils. A smoky coal-burning stove gave a little warmth in winter, but children often had to stop work, stand and do exercises to warm up. In summer, however, the classroom could become hot and stifling, as the inspector of Stirchley School found.

✿ What did the government inspector think was wrong with Stirchley School? How did he hope to improve things?

Stirchley School Inspector's Report, 1890

'The ventilation of the rooms would be improved by putting ventilating shafts in the roof. The classroom in which the infants are taught is so crowded that it is with considerable hesitation that I recommend payment of the grant. Care must be taken in future that the average attendance does not exceed the limits prescribed by Article 96 (a) or the next grant may be withheld without further warning.'

A spelling lesson. Desks had tilting lids with shelves below for slates.

WHAT EQUIPMENT DID CHILDREN USE?

Unlike the bright tables of today, Victorian school desks were made of dark varnished wood. Often they had lifting lids, with space for books inside. On the top was a china ink well for liquid ink, a groove for a pencil, and perhaps a hook on the side for hanging a slate when not in use.

Younger children learned to write on slates using a thin stick of slate called a slate pencil. Sometimes the slates came from house roofs. They were usually framed in wood to prevent them breaking. Paper was expensive, but a slate could be used over and over again after being wiped with a damp rag. Sometimes children spat on their slates and rubbed them with their fingers – but this was frowned on, as it could spread infections. To help with maths, the teacher used a large abacus – coloured beads were moved along to show addition and subtraction of numbers. Some schools had a small abacus for each child to use.

Most children learned to write using a slate and pencil.

This Victorian boy's chemistry set was intended for use at home, not school.

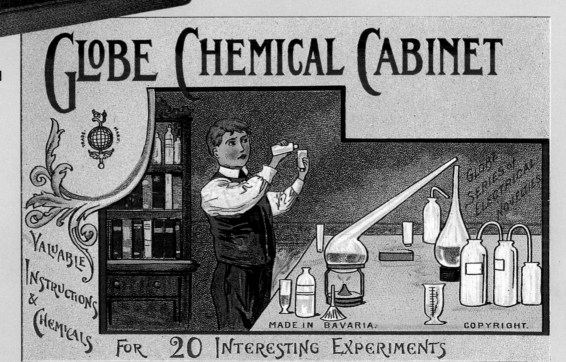

GLOBE CHEMICAL CABINET

TRADE MARK

GLOBE "SERIES" OF ELECTRICAL NOVELTIES

VALUABLE INSTRUCTIONS & CHEMICALS

MADE IN BAVARIA.

COPYRIGHT.

FOR 20 INTERESTING EXPERIMENTS

Pupils in the senior standards were occasionally allowed to use paper, either with lead pencils or ink pens. The 'ink monitor' mixed the ink (from a powder) and poured a little into each child's ink well. The nibs were scratchy, and it was hard to avoid blobs and blots, even if this risked a caning. Children learned to form their letters by copying words from books called copy-books, so they all wrote in exactly the same way.

❧ What do you notice about the floor level of the classroom shown here?

❧ Why do you think this was sometimes necessary?

These girls are crammed into long rows of narrow desks.

DETECTIVE WORK

Ask your local museum for a photocopy of a page from a Victorian handwriting copy-book. Have a go at filling it in with an ink pen. In what ways is this style of writing different from your normal writing?

Sometimes, lessons meant walking in the fields for nature study, or looking at things taken from an 'object box'. This had compartments with lots of tiny objects that could be passed round and touched. The box might contain anything from fossils or dried leaves to samples of different fabrics. Children must have looked forward to their weekly object lesson.

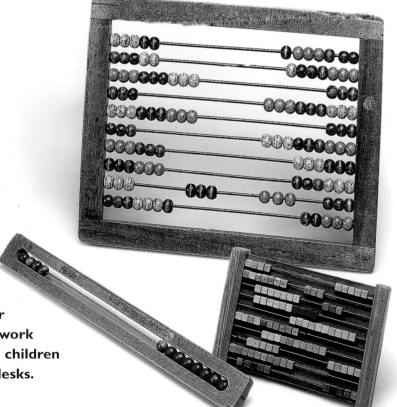

The abacus helped children with number work. The teacher showed them how to work something out with the big abacus. Then children used the smaller versions on their own desks.

WHEN DID PUPILS STUDY LITERACY AND NUMERACY?

The whole of the Explanations, Actions and Emendations, the Original Music, and the Original Poetry in Parts I., II., and III. of this work are the Compiler's own, and are Copyright.

THE INFANT RECITATION BOOK.

(Part III.)

No. 101.   LITTLE BY LITTLE.

One step and then another,
    And the longest walk is ended;
One stitch and then another,
    And the largest rent is mended;
One flake upon another,
    And the deepest snow is laid;
One brick upon another,
    And the highest wall is made.

No. 102.   BATHING.

He didn't like bathing, oh dear! oh dear!
The sea was so cold, and the waves came so near,
But sister was gentle, oh, sister was kind,
She whispered of beautiful shells they would find,
She told him the waves sing a wonderful song,
That only to wavelets and ripplets belong.
"So will you not bathe, and come with me
And learn, if you can, the song of the sea?"
Then slowly the frown faded out of his face,
And a smile like a ripple came back in its place.

No. 103.   THE LITTLE COOK.

Oh, I can make a pancake,
    And I can toss it high,
And I can cook a mutton chop,
    And I can make a pie;
Oh, I could do so many things,
    If only I might try!

But I can't learn my spelling,
    And I can't do my sums—
Still, I can make a pudding,

And I can stone the plums,
For I have useful little fingers
    And clever little thumbs.

I wonder why to do such things
    Mamma won't let me try,
And says that birds must learn to
    Before they try to fly.   [walk
I'm not a bird—I long to cook,
    And so for that I sigh.

A book of poems. Children learned them by heart and recited them out loud.

DETECTIVE WORK

Hunt in a second-hand bookshop or charity shop for old reading books that were used by Victorian children. Compare them with your favourite storybooks and note down some differences in the illustrations and the vocabulary used. Are there any other differences?

Most of the time! However, in Victorian schools, literacy and numeracy were usually referred to as 'the three Rs'. This stood for 'Reading, wRiting and aRithmetic'. Children had to master the three Rs before using them to study other subjects.

Today, we know that people learn to read in different ways. But Victorian children all began by learning the alphabet. Then they put letters together to form simple one-syllable words. The whole class would chant together, 'M – A – T spells MAT'. Once they knew these words, they were taught to add letters, so MAT grew into MATTER and so on. Some children soon fell behind, while others were held back. Victorian children were not encouraged to learn at their own speed.

Most schools had few reading books, so the same readers were used over and over again. They were not colourfully illustrated, and pupils soon lost interest in the stories. In many schools, the Bible was the main reading book. Inspectors often tested children by asking them to read out passages. With long words and old-fashioned language, this was not a very fair test.

A cartoon of W E Forster, who in 1870 recommended that all children should learn to read and write.

❧ In the cartoon, do most adults seem to care about the children's education?

❧ What makes W E Forster seem different?

In arithmetic, too, everyone had to learn at the same pace. This usually involved learning times tables and lists of money, weights and measures. These were said aloud over and over again until children knew them by heart. If the teacher asked, 'How much does a bushel of wheat weigh?' a child would answer, 'Fifty-six pounds, sir,' without having to think about it. The Victorians used 'imperial' weights and measures such as bushels, pecks, chains, rods, perches, stones, pounds and ounces. These were hard to learn, and even harder to add up, divide or multiply.

The sum in this boy's maths book shows the difficulty of multiplying money in pounds, shillings and pence.

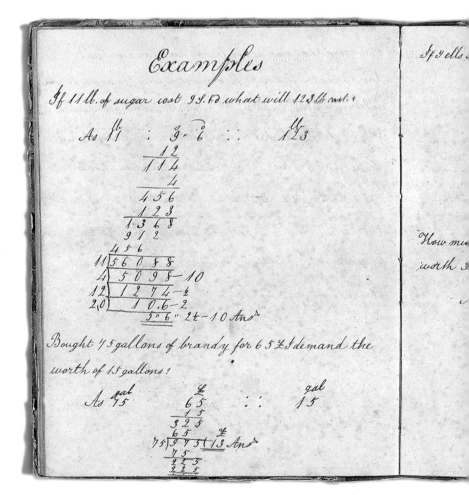

WHAT ELSE WAS ON THE TIMETABLE?

It was the Victorian head teacher's job to draw up the school timetable. The timetable shown on this page was written in 1872. The day began with scripture – a lesson about the Bible. On Fridays, there was catechism instead, when children learned by heart answers to questions about their religion. Barnham Broom, like most Victorian schools, belonged to the Church, so religion was taken very seriously. After religious instruction, the rest of every morning was spent on the three Rs.

This timetable was used in a Norfolk village school in the 1870s. It was found stuck inside an old picture.

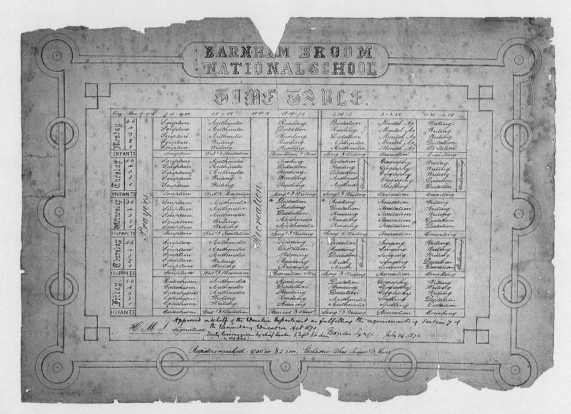

The school day was usually divided in two. At Barnham Broom there was a long break from midday until 2.10 pm. There were no school meals (these did not start until the Second World War in 1939), so children needed enough time to walk home for lunch. Afternoon school was a little more varied, depending on which standard pupils were in. But, as they were all taught in the same classroom, all pupils studied recitation (Wednesday) and singing (Thursday) together. On Tuesdays and Fridays, older pupils studied geography while the younger ones learned spellings.

Schools sometimes taught other subjects, too. Boys might learn carpentry skills while girls had needlework lessons. They practised different stitches by making miniature shirts and dresses. Science was taught in some boys' grammar schools. Even history and geography were not compulsory, though schools could claim extra money from the government if they taught them well. History involved memorizing dates and facts, mainly about kings and queens, whilst geography meant copying down the names of places shown on a map or globe.

Singing lessons

Children sometimes sang this song at school. The tune was the same as *God Save The Queen*.

*'God Save our Gracious Land,
May heaven's protecting hand
Still guard our shore;
May peace her power extend,
Foe be transformed to friend,
And Britain's rights depend
On war no more.'*

Whatever the subject, the method was the same. The teacher wrote something on the blackboard, and the children copied it. They learned it off by heart, and were tested by the teacher. Victorian schools did not aim to stir the imagination!

Some older girls at a 'higher grade' school had science lessons.

DETECTIVE WORK

See if your local library or museum have any old school textbooks and compare them with the ones you use today. The library or Record Office may have copies of school adverts or prospectuses that show you what subjects the children were taught.

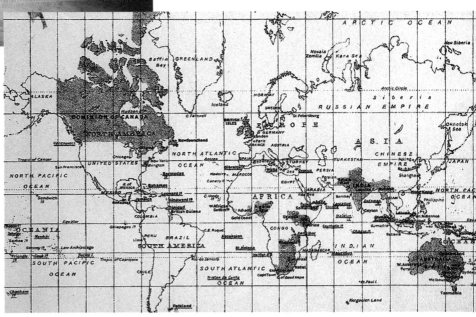

The British Empire was marked in red for geography lessons.

DID CHILDREN GET ANY EXERCISE?

A favourite saying in Victorian times was 'a healthy mind in a healthy body', and schools tried to put this into practice. They wanted their pupils to be physically fit so that their minds would be alert and active too. Sports and team games were especially popular at the fee-paying private schools.

Some schools had their own games. 'Fives' was a ball game played at Eton College. But football, said one headmaster, was 'a vulgar activity fit only for butchers' boys and farm labourers'. Despite this, most public schools played some form of football, though often with very different rules. At Rugby School, the rules allowed boys to pick up the ball and run with it. The idea caught on, and the new game of 'rugby football' eventually became a national sport.

Team games were not usually played at elementary schools attended by poorer children. However, from 1871 the government encouraged all schools to include some physical exercise in the weekly timetable. This was usually 'drill'. Like soldiers on parade grounds, the children waved their arms or legs, jogged, lifted weights or marched on the spot in time to whistle blows or orders barked out by the teacher. Most pupils hated drill. But, for the teachers it was an easy way to exercise a large number of children in a small space. It also taught pupils to obey orders at once, without thinking – so it helped to create discipline.

DETECTIVE WORK

At your local reference library, find out about playground games, especially those involving rhymes. Look up the origins of games such as rugby football, fives and lacrosse to discover what types of school these were first played in.

This boy was allowed to play with his hoop during breaks from lessons.

Squeezed into their desks, silently scratching at their slates, Victorian children must have watched the clock and longed for break time. For a few precious minutes, hoops and skipping ropes appeared, there were games of catch, the playground became a football pitch or hopscotch was chalked on the ground. Some pupils kept marbles or tiddlywinks in their pockets, while others hid catapults or conkers, hoping that they would not be caught. It was often the playground as much as the classroom where friendships were made and lost, ideas and opinions were formed, and children learned about the world and their place in it.

Girls doing drill in the playground of a London school.

✤ Compare the two pictures on this page. How much space is needed for each activity?

✤ Why was it difficult to play team games at schools for poor children?

A game of rugby football at Rugby School, where the game was invented.

YOUR PROJECT

Have you followed the Detective Work activities in this book? If so, you should now be able to track down enough clues to produce your own project about Victorian schools. First, decide on a topic to investigate. Choose something that you find really interesting. You could get some ideas by looking through this book's index. You could also use one of the following questions as a starting point.

Topic Questions
- Where are your nearest Victorian school buildings? Are they still used today? How have they changed?
- How many types of schools were there in your area during Victorian times? What sort of children went to each school?
- What can we find out from looking at photos of Victorian children in school?
- What makes Victorian school books and classroom equipment different from their modern equivalents?
- How did a Victorian teacher's job differ from that of a teacher today?

The Victorian schoolroom at the Weald and Downland Museum in Sussex.

Children at Gressenhall School, Norfolk, in about 1890. The boys with short hair and no ties came from the local workhouse.

You also need to think about how to present your project. Here are a few ideas.

Project Presentation
- Draw a map of your area to show where the schools were in Victorian times.
- Write an imaginary diary of your life as a Victorian school pupil. Base your story on real incidents from school log books and other sources.
- Practise writing with an ink pen and include some examples of your own Victorian-style handwriting in your project.
- Write up some information about an event in history, in the form of a Victorian school textbook. Include questions and answers for pupils to learn by heart.
- Illustrate your project with photocopies of photos of Victorian schoolchildren or buildings.

You might find something quite unusual for your project. Sherlock produced a project about workhouse schools. He discovered that poor children who were sent to workhouses often had a better schooling than those who lived at home with their families. Sherlock found that workhouse children learned reading and writing in the mornings, and had practical lessons like tailoring and shoe-mending in the afternoons. He read about a 12-year-old workhouse boy called William Rush who took over the running of his school when the teacher was sick. Later, William trained as a teacher and went to work in another workhouse school.

GLOSSARY

abacus A counting frame with coloured beads.

assaulted Attacked, or hit.

British schools Elementary church schools run by 'non-conformists' like Methodists and Congregationalists.

bushel A measure of volume, equal to 8 gallons (36.4 litres).

catechism Questions and answers about Christianity which children had to learn.

cripples Slang term for people with disabilities.

directories Books with lists of information about people or places.

elementary schools Schools for poor children aged under 14.

grammar schools Schools for older pupils where they learned Latin and prepared for university.

log books Books in which the head teacher had to write down what happened each day.

monitor An older pupil who was put in charge of teaching younger ones.

national schools Elementary schools run by the Church of England.

private schools Fee-paying schools run for profit by their owners.

Sabbath Sunday – 'the Lord's Day'.

ANSWERS

page 5
☙ The thing that made these schools different was money. The plain schoolroom at the top is crowded with simply dressed poor children. But the public school below has grand old buildings and smartly dressed, rich scholars.

page 6
☙ This is the old lady's living room, with a fireplace, cooking equipment, kitchen cupboard and table.

☙ No, the furniture is unsuitable for a school. There are no desks, so most of the children have to stand for their lessons.

page 8
☙ The pictures show fifteen different ways to sit or stand at a desk. Sherlock shows you a sixteenth!

☙ Discipline was strict. When the teacher called a number, the children had to sit or stand exactly like the picture with that number.

page 11
☙ The teacher on page 10 rewarded the children by displaying their work on the classroom walls. The one on page 11 frightened the children by hitting them if they made mistakes.

☙ The children on the left probably enjoyed their lessons and therefore did better work.

page 13
☙ Modern children would find working in old weights, measures and money very difficult.

☙ Yes, the inspector had to hear every child read and then inspected their copy-books.

page 15

- They needed handkerchiefs to blow their noses without spreading germs to each other.
- No, this meant the way that pages curled up at the edges. They looked like a dog's ears.

page 17

- Teaching was a hard job. Classes were large and some children were hard to control.

page 19

- The inspector said that the school was stuffy and overcrowded. He threatened to stop paying the government grant if this was not put right.

page 21

- The floor slopes up to the back of the room.
- Classes were so big that it was hard for all the children to see the teacher.

page 23

- Most of the adults appear more interested in each other than in the children.
- W E Forster is the only one who listens to what the children have to say.

page 27

- Drill needs only a small space to exercise many children, but football and rugby need a large space for a few children.
- Schools for poor children did not have enough space to play team games.

Books to Read

You Wouldn't Want to be A Victorian Schoolchild
by John Malam (Hodder Wayland, 2002)

Who? What? When? Victorians
by Bob Fowke (Hodder Wayland, 2003)

Life in Victorian Times: Home and School
by Neil Morris (Belitha Press 1999)

Places to visit

The Victorian School of the 3 Rs
Parade Street, Llangollen, North Wales

Weald and Downland Open Air Museum
Singleton, Chichester, West Sussex PO18 0EU

INDEX

Numbers in **bold** refer to pictures and captions.